CAGE *of*
FIREFLIES

BOOKS BY LUCIEN STRYK

Taproot
The Trespasser
Zen: Poems, Prayers, Sermons, Anecdotes, Interviews
Notes for a Guidebook
Heartland: Poets of the Midwest
World of the Buddha: An Introduction to Buddhist Literature
The Pit and Other Poems
Afterimages: Zen Poems of Shinkichi Takahashi
Twelve Death Poems of the Chinese Zen Masters
Zen Poems of China and Japan: The Crane's Bill
Awakening
Heartland II: Poets of the Midwest
Three Zen Poems
Selected Poems
Haiku of the Japanese Masters
The Duckweed Way: Haiku of Issa
The Penguin Book of Zen Poetry
The Duckpond
Prairie Voices: Poets of Illinois
Zen Poems
Encounter with Zen: Writings on Poetry and Zen
Cherries
Bird of Time: Haiku of Basho
Willows
Collected Poems 1953–1983
On Love and Barley: Haiku of Basho
Triumph of the Sparrow: Zen Poems of Shinkichi Takahashi
Bells of Lombardy
Of Pen and Ink and Paper Scraps
The Dumpling Field: Haiku of Issa
The Gift of Great Poetry
Cage of Fireflies: Modern Japanese Haiku

CAGE of FIREFLIES

Modern Japanese Haiku

translated by Lucien Stryk

Swallow Press
Ohio University Press
Athens

Swallow Press/Ohio University Press books are printed on acid-free paper ∞

97   96   95   94   93   5   4   3   2   1

Library of Congress Cataloging-in-Publication Data

Cage of fireflies : modern Japanese haiku / translated by Lucian Stryk.
    p.   cm.
   ISBN 0-8040-0976-7 (cloth). — ISBN 0-8040-0977-5 (pbk.)
   1. Haiku—Translations into English. 2. Japanese poetry—1868—
Translations into English. 3. Haiku—History and criticism.
I. Stryk, Lucien.
PL782.E3C34   1993   93-15212
895.6′14408—dc20   CIP

NOTE

In 1975, five years before his death, Takashi Ikemoto and I completed the manuscript of what was to become, in 1977, *The Penguin Book of Zen Poetry*. An important part of the book was made up of haiku, and we translated a great many that both of us loved, especially those of haiku's "great four," Basho (1644-94), Buson (1715-83), Issa (1763-1827) and Shiki (1867-1902). We wound up with far too many, given the purpose of the collection, so we left out all material by twentieth-century poets. In 1985 I was in Japan again, to work, with the assistance of Noboru Fujiwara, on a book of Issa's haiku. Two years after Noboru Fujiwara's death, in 1991, this collection was published as *The Dumpling Field: Haiku of Issa*. While I was working on the Issa book with Noboru Fujiwara, he asked me to translate with him some pieces by his haiku master, and leader of the Tenro Haiku School, Seishi Yamaguchi. I found myself becoming increasingly interested in modern haiku, and while reworking the pieces done with Takashi Ikemoto, and with the Seishi Yamaguchi poems in hand, I thought I might put together a modern collection one day. The day has come, and *Cage of Fireflies: Modern Japanese Haiku* is the result, a book which could not have been done without the assistance of my good friends, to whose memory it is dedicated. Because he lived into the twentieth century, and had such a profound effect on the poets of his time, Shiki's poems begin the book. For permission to use them, I am grateful to Penguin Books (London, England), publisher of *The Penguin Book of Zen Poetry*, and for permission to use the introduction I thank *American Poetry Review* and *London Magazine*.

In this poor body, composed of one hundred bones and nine openings, is something called spirit, a flimsy curtain swept this way and that by the slightest breeze. It is spirit, such as it is, which led me to poetry, at first little more than a pastime, then the full business of my life. There have been times when my spirit, so dejected, almost gave up the quest, other times when it was proud, triumphant. So it has been from the very start, never finding peace with itself, always doubting the worth of what it makes. . . .

—BASHO, *The Records of a Travel-Worn Satchel*

CONTENTS

INTRODUCTION

I. CAGE OF FIREFLIES

Into the cage of
fireflies, mostly dead,
I send a breath.

— KASHO

Each year as darkness comes alive with sparkles, I
remember the night my son handed me a jar of wilting fire-
flies, confident that I could turn their glow back on. I hadn't
come across the poet Kasho yet. I wish I had, for this poem
on a cage of fireflies might have offset a small boy's disap-
pointment in his father.

· · ·

Great poets of all cultures, including the haiku poets of
Japan, are strongly emotional, moving constantly from light
to dark and seeking change. Since art's beginning there have
been some who have emerged with a clear mission to revolu-
tionize current practice, stand things on their heads. In the
history of haiku such were Basho (1644-94), and a couple of
hundred years later, Shiki (1867-1902), among haiku's "Great
Four," the others being Buson (1715-83), equally known as a
painter, and Issa (1763-1827), perhaps Japan's drollest, most
tender and loved poet. Basho and Shiki shook the art to its
foundations.

1

Before Basho haiku was largely a dilettantish fashion for the idle. He set about transforming an art for which, from youth, he had a passion, and would from time to time, especially in his remarkable *haibun* (mix of prose and haiku), comment on its aesthetics. Fortunately there were admirers farseeing enough to record his words. We owe much to Doho, for example, for inking this snatch of conversation:

> The master said, "Learn about a pine tree from a pine tree, and about a bamboo stalk from a bamboo stalk." What he meant was that the poet should detach his mind from self . . . and enter into the object, sharing its delicate life and its feelings. Whereupon a poem forms of itself. Description of the object is not enough: unless a poem contains feelings which have come from the object, the object and the poet's self will be separate things.

How profound, at the awakening of new haiku, such comments must have seemed. Few of Basho's disciples, who grew rapidly in number, had prepared themselves as he had done through Zen discipline (he was to become a monk) for so deep an immersion into nature. Though he could on occasion be scathingly dismissive of the work of earlier poets, Sogi (1421–1502), Sokan (1458–1546), Moritake (1472–1549), yet he honored them for having created haiku, breaking up the *haikai renga*, sequences of seventeen-syllable verses composed by poets writing together in turn. It was by then a tradition of two hundred years, and it was they who started it.

Tradition in the arts is highly complex. Take music. The pianist of today performs not just a Mozart sonata, but also in a sense those pianists who learned from each other since his time. Without each interpretation handed on, establishing an ultimate performance, the score would be mere notes played any which-way. Something of the kind is true of poetry, all poetry. The emotions and insights the first poets wished to express were, by their intuitively arrived at practice, given forms, which henceforth, up to the present, proved themselves important factors of the art. Basho was as much the son of Sogi,

Sokan and Moritake, and those who followed, as their most probing critic. From them he learned the basics, that it was possible to compress within seventeen harmoniously ordered syllables feelings and insights which meant most to him. What made him superior was a deeper sensibility and a subtler mind, making possible such all-encompassing essences as these:

Spring air —
woven moon
and plum scent.

Year's end,
all corners
of this floating world, swept.

To the willow —
all hatred, and desire
of your heart.

Basho forged what was to be accepted as the essential standard of the art. Soon others followed him, intimately binding themselves to nature, observing keenly, touching lightly, to the best of their ability emulating the master. One such was Kikaku (1661-1707):

Full autumn moon —
on the straw mat,
pine shadow.

Leaf
of the yam —
raindrop's world.

The raindrop's world is the world of all true haiku. These poets were fully aware of the physical, and it is this absorption which may be the source of their greatest strength. Nothing too high, too low, they write most lovingly of things which by most are unloved. Hear Issa:

Clouds of mosquitoes —
it would be bare
without them.

In my house
mice and fireflies
get along.

And Buson:

On the iris,
kite's
soft droppings.

Swallows,
in eaves of mansions,
of hovels.

In the West, from the time of the Imagists in the early years
of the century to the present, it has been the stunning economy,
the particularity of haiku which has had greatest appeal, but
in the finest examples there is something above, beyond keen
observation: full disclosure of the poet's sensibility, within the
smallest space. Take this poem by Lady Chiyo-Jo (1701-75):

In the well-bucket,
a morning glory —
I borrow water.

And this by Lady Sute-Jo (1633-98):

Woman —
how hot the skin
she covers.

Despite avoidance, for the most part, of poetic devices thought
essential in the West — metaphor, simile, personification — haiku

are still able to deal with the most human concerns. With few or no adjectives or adverbs the poet is able to give sharpest perceptions, startling revelations. That which for years we may have bypassed, ignored is suddenly illuminated, thus better prized as the remarkable thing it has always been:

Nightingale —
my clogs
stick in the mud.
— BONCHO (?-1714)

Barn's burnt down —
now
I can see the moon.
— MASAHIDE (1657-1723)

On encountering such poems by his contemporaries, one can't help wondering to what degree they might have been inspired by Basho. It is quite probable that these poets learned from him how a few words could cover so large a range, might express one's life. One thing is indisputable: before Basho such poems were not written, as if nature lay dormant until he came along to point to its very heart.

Attempting to give an idea of the way haiku works, without making cultural comparisons, I have often cited the American poet Ezra Pound's "In a Station of the Metro," a most admired haiku-like poem:

The apparition of these faces in the crowd;
Petals on a wet, black bough.

A simile, almost as startling as haiku, yet much of what is said would to a haiku poet be implied. Incorporating the title (haiku are not titled), he might make the poem read:

Faces in the metro —
petals
on a wet black bough.

If asked why, he might say that the first few words, "The apparition of these," though sonorous enough, contribute nothing. Nor does the word "crowd," metro stations usually being crowded — and yes, the "petals" of the simile suggest that. His version, he might state, transforms the piece into acceptable haiku, one rather like, perhaps less effective than, Onitsura's:

> Autumn wind —
> across the fields,
> faces.

Without using simile, Onitsura stuns with an immediacy of vision: faces whipped by a cold wind.

Modern haiku, the province of this collection, began with the last of haiku's Great Four, Shiki, whose impact on the art came close to Basho's. Born in 1867, he died at thirty-five, in 1902. Indefatigably pursuing the art, in spite of being ravaged by tuberculosis, he quickly established himself as a master. He sent out shock waves by dismissing virtually all earlier haiku, including Basho's, though conceding reluctantly that perhaps one-fifth of the poet's work was good. From the beginning he was out to make a difference, to let nothing, not even the most revered progenitor, stand in his way. He proclaimed, "A poem has no *meaning*. It is feeling alone." Iconoclastic, daring to a very great fault, he wasted little time establishing what was soon to be seen as a modern canon for the art.

Shiki's passion was proverbial. Like John Keats, knowing he was doomed to early death, he willed to make the most of his brief residence on earth. He had two great obsessions: haiku and persimmons — a doctor restricted him to two persimmons a day, but poems . . . he wrote thousands of which a surprising number have worn extremely well:

> Thing long forgotten —
> pot where a flower blooms,
> this spring day.

Autumn wind:
gods, Buddha —
lies, lies, lies.

Such silence:
snow tracing wings
of mandarin ducks.

Shiki had an unusual gift for articulating the most subtle aesthetic insights, always seriously and, when possible, publicly. He would divest haiku of the "sublime," seeking constantly the "richness of the plain." To make clear, he used such common terms as *heitan* (flatness), *heii* (plainness), *tanpaku* (lightness) and *jūnj* (ordinariness) — hardly as elegant or imaginative as Basho, who used the term *karumi* for "lightness," and was to state that "a good poem is one in which the form of the verse and the joining of its parts seem light as a shallow river flowing over its sandy bed." Shiki was ready at all times to send down directives to his growing band of disciples: "Don't think — feel. Be natural." "Get your ideas not from past 'classical' haiku, but from the everyday world." "Eliminate every inessential word, down to the bone." "Write from your feelings, and only for yourself. If you feel strongly, so will your reader."

Among the poet's major contributions to haiku aesthetic were his very original concepts, *shasei* and *makoto*, which because of their importance to those who followed him must be defined. *Shasei*, simply put, is realism, and means copying the subject, but selectively, emphasizing elements most characteristic. He gave the following example: a red camellia blooming in dark woods would strike one as especially beautiful in haiku if the darkness of the woods were emphasized, and the flower described as briefly as possible. The Tenro Haiku School, led by Seishi Yamaguchi, holds *shasei* as virtual creed, and speaks of it as on-the-spot composition with the subject "traced to its origin."

By *makoto* Shiki meant *shasei* directed toward "inner reality," with the same concentration on the direct rendering of subject, but the subject being the poet's self. The self is experienced as objectively as anything in nature. More than anything, perhaps, *makoto* is "truthful feeling," and as members of Soun, and other haiku schools, would have it, Significance. Because *makoto* naturally leads to a focusing on revelations of spirit, the poet may write less than those practicing *shasei* alone. That is to be expected, as it would be anywhere. *Makoto* may also lead, at times, to flaunting of formal elements, including as in the case of Soun poets the syllabic restrictions. Soun is sometimes called the "free-verse" school, its freedom legitimized by precedent in Shiki himself, who wrote many poems of more, or less, than seventeen syllables.

Shasei and *makoto* are surely among the most important contributions Shiki was to make to haiku, and he was tireless in expressing views on them and other matters, at times on the most practical and basic level. He wrote a haiku column for the newspaper *Nippon*, and in 1896, in order to distinguish his group from other larger groups, he published nothing less than a manifesto. His group, he wrote, based their poems on emotion, avoided triteness, despised wordiness, used any and all kinds of language, from that of ancient court poetry to modern slang, so long as the words harmonized tonally, and finally he insisted on their independence from all special schools and lineages. A poet was to be respected solely for the quality of his work. Shiki more than implied that other groups were wanting in such matters; he openly castigated them.

Shiki's favorite of all past poets was Buson, and he was at times extravagant in praising the poet-painter, in awe of his startling work, so full of color and imagination, with a vocabulary richer than that of all others. He once stated, with characteristic boldness, that of ten Buson poems seven or eight were superb, whereas the better known and adulated Basho had only two or three good pieces out of ten. That was a staggering judgment, striking many as not only wrong-headed but sourly ungenerous. Yet he persisted, saying such claims were "for the good of the art."

The ideal modern haiku, in Shiki's view, is written in *around* seventeen syllables, with, as in the past, a "season word." Such a view, while hardly severe, was held provocative by traditionalists, whereas it was applauded, and adopted, by others, who took comfort in the thought that the value of a poem is its individuality and freedom from stereotypes. The ideal poem is fresh and uninhibited, haiku rather than *hokku* of the past. There may be justice in the fact that Shiki was the first to employ regularly the term haiku: those who gathered around him were challenged and inspired by his example. By writing true haiku they hoped to prove themselves his worthy followers.

One of Shiki's most illustrious fellow poets, and exact contemporary (both were born in 1867), was Soseki, who was to become a novelist — *Kokoro* (1914) is one of Japan's great novels. Yet like other haiku poets who also wrote fiction, Akutagawa (*Rashomon*) among them, his abiding love was poetry. How well Soseki understood the nature of the new haiku:

Winter song —
hatchet felling bamboos
in the mountains.

Echoing
the autumn stream,
a driven stake.

Akutagawa shows equal understanding:

Winter wind —
sardine's still
ocean-colored.

White chrysanthemums —
light/dark,
even their smell.

Akutagawa died by his own hand at thirty-five, and fifty years later, through Akira Kurosawa's film based on his stories, *Rashomon*, he would achieve worldwide fame. One can only hope that he had many moments wonderful as those poems.

Toward the end of his life, confined to a sickbed, Shiki often reflected on his tempestuous youth, expressing regret for outbursts and harsh judgments. At such times he would concede his comments on Basho had been particularly unfortunate, yet he insisted someone had to do what he had done — for an art to which he had devoted the best of his hours. It had been in danger of suffocating, he had arrived in the nick of time.

In the West, used as we are to upheavals in the arts, and the dramatic impact of powerful personalities, we find it difficult to appreciate how socially imprudent can be the flaunting of norms in a culture convention-bound as Japan's. (Even now, in a city modern as Kyoto, it is considered virtually criminal for a pedestrian to cross against the light, even when no cars are present.) The great Zen poet Shinkichi Takahashi (1901–87) was jailed from time to time as a youth for just such "impulsive behavior." Yet nothing stopped him living as Zennist:

> My hair's falling fast —
> this afternoon
> I'm off to Asia Minor.

In order to give fuller vision of his special world, perhaps, Shinkichi Takahashi turned to free-verse, rather in the way that Soseki and Akutagawa turned to fiction.

Shiki, on the other hand, would have found it impossible, though he did write impressive *tanka* (the thirty-one-syllable form), to abandon haiku, and because as a maturing artist he would from time to time feel the constraints of a form so short, he invented *rensaku*, or "sequential composition." *Rensaku* has been especially favored in recent years by the Tenro School, and it is not unusual for its members to gather at a given spot, often a Zen temple garden, and write as many as one hundred haiku on a chosen theme or set of objects. Shiki claimed that through *rensaku* the poet would be able to explore feelings too complex, perhaps, for a single haiku, and just as in sequential composition in the West — among the most important being T. S. Eliot's "The Waste Land" — he might through careful modulation and arrangement of parts give the work greater breadth and complexity, a vision more complete.

Rensaku may very well be regarded as Shiki's most unusual contribution to haiku, possibly conceived to give the art the scope and modernity of much Western poetry he knew and greatly admired. His own *rensaku*, just as his individual poems, established him firmly as one of haiku's Great Four. Of the four his life was shortest, but hardly least eventful. One of the best-read poets of his day, he became increasingly hopeful of demonstrating the worth of haiku internationally, and all his experiments were conducted with that serious purpose in mind. It is tantalizing to imagine what he might have accomplished had he been allowed a full measure of years. One thing would surely have pleased him greatly: around a decade after his death the Imagist School of poetry was established in London by Ezra Pound and others, and as a major element of its credo, a key factor of its aesthetic, was the need of bringing into English and American poetry the qualities of haiku, especially its terseness and its sensitivity to nature. The poems in *Cage of Fireflies*, led by Shiki, offer ample proof of haiku's continuing vitality.

· · ·

I am listening as I write to a recording of the contemporary Japanese composer Toru Takemitsu's "Raintree," a piece for percussion. The composer, much interviewed and discussed these days, often speaks of an indebtedness to Zen and haiku. On my study wall hangs an old mask, which was used in Noh plays in Japan. Facing it there's another prized possession, "Plum Blossom," a *sumie* (ink painting) by the eighteenth-century painter Ike-no-Taiga, who trained in Zen with one of the most illustrious masters in the history of the sect, Hakuin, and formed a close friendship with the poet-painter most revered by Shiki, and another of haiku's Great Four, Buson. The two collaborated in 1771 on a remarkable album of paintings "Juben Ju-gi" (Ten Conveniences and Ten Enjoyments of Rural Living), and were regarded as the two masters of *Nanga*, or

Southern Style, painting, also called *Bunjin-ga*, or Literati painting. Perhaps I might be excused for wondering if Ike-no-Taiga had ever shown Buson his "Plum Blossom." Music, drama, painting, and poetry, all of a piece in Japan's unique culture, and all quite beyond the spoilage of time.

Though it is true that Shiki's radical dismissal of haiku's past led to the art's rejuvenation (as Basho's had done before him), the poems herein show that haiku is today, essentially, what at its best it has always been. As in Basho's time the modern poet takes a natural, a most ordinary event, and without fuss, ornament or inflated words makes of it a rarest moment — sparely rendered, crystallized, a microcosm, which can reveal transcendent unity. Small wonder that people throughout the world have come to care for haiku.

The wind has shaken free the last drops from Toru Takemitsu's "Raintree," the Ike-no-Taiga scroll "Plum Blossom" illuminates the hours, as it has done for well over two hundred years, and haiku will remain through the ages, rekindled from time to time, as if by a breath sent into a cage of mostly dying fireflies.

II. MEETING AT HAGI-NO-TERA

When very young, in Chicago, I thought I saw a miracle in Soldier Field. Holding tight to my father's hand, I gaped as Auguste Piccard climbed into the gondola of a giant balloon and waved (I was sure, at me). The balloon rose, becoming smaller as it drifted, disappeared. Little did I know that lift-off would one day touch down into a poem. From that time on I heard of other miracles, machines of one sort or another making life easier for all, releasing minds from drudgery, making time for finer things — art, music, theatre, dance, poetry. Such fancies did not last, for I discovered as all must that machines often make people expendable. Since the industrial revolution, war's efficiency has accelerated, and in our own time rainforests and wildlife are threatened, soup lines lengthen, the homeless multiply. Bitter conflicts fester in all corners of the earth, children murder children in drug wars, and there are drastic cutbacks in funds for education. Will the artists be the first to go? Who then will be left to record voices, colors, sounds of our generation as so faithfully recorded for us in the past?

In these days of unrest I think of an autumn day, some years ago, back in Japan, when I boarded a train with two friends in the industrial city of Osaka, and stepped out into the fresh breeze of Sone. The day was clear and cool, and we strolled by toylike shop fronts, patchworked with rice-crackers, dried sardines, bright fruits and vegetables, scarves, kites — all sorts of things. We turned down a street of red-tiled roofs behind high walls, passed through a deserted lane into the garden of Hagi-no-Tera, a Zen temple on the outskirts of the village. The garden, renowned for autumn flowering and for its dedication to poetry, seemed a bit overgrown, perhaps left that way with deliberate nonchalance. Among clumps of chrysanthemums, bronze, white, purple, gold, were conical stone monuments engraved with poems exalting flowers, some by Basho (1644–94), Buson (1715–83), Issa (1763–1827) and Shiki (1867–1902), the "great four" of haiku. As afternoon sun filtered through the pines fringing the garden, we walked slowly by the memorial stones, through shadows of lanterns on the path, passed haikuists absorbed in note-taking, and talked of poems and poets. Caught up in the aura of the place, our voices became whispers, and we turned to quiet contemplation. Pondering the art of masters, each so spunkily his own man, I dared to mull over their communion, as if their spirits wakened and they met up, crosslegged on the grass, for a chat over a flask of *sake*.

Basho (raising his cup): *Kampai!* Long have I felt the spirit of your presence, your every line beaming into haiku buffs come here from all over. They tend to lump us together, like these petals on chrysanthemum heads, yet . . .

Buson: Your "yet"? I too have cocked an ear.

Shiki: I'm suspicious of that "yet."

Issa: You would be, Shiki, having taken liberties, dismissing much of Basho's work. Speaking for myself, I find it more than tolerant of him to knock one back with you. Some can't speak well of anyone.

Shiki: I'm no idolator, like a few I could mention. No time to hand round compliments. Too little time, too much to . . .

Buson: If I may barge in, Shiki, I've long wanted to thank you for kind words on my behalf. Excessive maybe, since my *cup of tea* was painting — no pun intended on your pen name, Issa.

Shiki: But when all's said and done, who could come close to your:
> A sudden chill —
> in our room my dead wife's
> comb, underfoot.

Buson: That was a lucky moment for me. How about your:
> Such silence:
> snow tracing wings
> of mandarin ducks.

Issa: Ah, but can lines anywhere compare with Basho's:
> Summer grasses,
> all that remains
> of soldiers' dreams.

Basho: My loyal friend, what of your tender yet amusing:
> I'm leaving —
> now you can make love,
> my flies.

There is much laughter, as *sake* is poured.

Shiki: Hold it, we're sounding like some mutual admiration society! We can do better in such stimulating company. I wonder who would look into the face of a chrysanthemum to clear the mind these days?

Basho: You no doubt spied the last group, pens in hand, gathering about us. Sad fate for such an art . . .

Issa: Such outpourings! No soul. Did you hear them render that piece by one, Tota:
> After hateful words,
> I roar off
> like a motorcycle.

Shiki: Hold it! You're speaking of a world you're hardly familiar with, my world. Given your background . . . I'll bet that dinky town of yours has never to this moment heard a train whistle. Kashiwabara — hardly on the map! How would you know . . .

Issa: What have machines to do with human condition, heart? That is the true province of haiku.

Buson: Issa, indeed your verse cuts to the very core — you are surely the most loved of all of us. Though you had little of love, and much suffering in your own time. But, hear me out, I speak as painter, artist, one not quick to confine any art to a given theme. It has form, color, it has — it had better have — pure harmony. I don't give a fig for an artist's heart, I want fruit of his eyes, his ears. Art could well do without sentiment.

Basho: Wait Buson, your pen is hardly free of it:
> In sudden flare
> of the mosquito wick,
> her flushed face.

Look here, you and Issa are more or less contemporaries, whereas Shiki and I, well, we come from different worlds. Is it surprising he dismissed, I think it was four-fifths, of my output, leaving little to admire! How many haiku did I compose, after all? A thousand? Whereas he, who lived fifteen fewer years than I, wrote twenty times as much. Let the world judge what is worthy.

Shiki: Come, Basho, you know full well you are regarded as Japan's greatest poet.

Basho: Yet you did your best to turn your generation from me. It shows up in their work. At least no one, not even you, accused me of rushing into print.

Shiki: Implying that's what I did?

Issa: I shouldn't butt in, but I poured out more than you, Shiki. True, I had more years—you died too young!—but my life was hardly less painful. I might say I am puzzled when the amateurs crowd round talking of your *shasei*, which, if I catch the meaning, gives them the license to write nonstop slap-dash drivel.

Shiki: That I resent. *Shasei, my shasei,* revived the art, which had outworn itself. Personally, I couldn't hang my washing out to dry like you. The things you're loved for, which you carry off so well, as . . . I'll hold my tongue.

Basho: A wise move. Do we descend to name calling? We, reasonable men? After all, there's room for everything, even "on the spot" composition, your *shasei.* "Tracing subjects to their origin" might well mean fresh seeing, just as in the practice of *zenkan,* pure seeing, which leads to stronger vision. To your credit, Shiki, you did start something! You see, I've learned from your disciples, and it's true you never promised anything significant would come of it. What does *shasei* really lead to? Haiku groups like Tenro, bearing notebooks, pens, scribbling in unison on anything in sight. Like that bunch over there, by Issa's stone.

Shiki: Any object? Why not? One's as good as another. What about Buson's:
> Dewy morn —
> these saucepans
> are beautiful.

Basho: Such a group around my saucepans would have dulled their shine! To create the miracle of art, well, it's a very personal thing. Takes contemplation, dignity, not crowds shuffling about — just watch them as they go by . . .

Buson: A poem is not only a miracle, but a problem seeking a solution. It has to be well shaped as any painting. Once on canvas it must stand up to serious appraisal. I'm sorry, Shiki, to me your *shasei* seems more political than aesthetic. An attempt to democratize art, which must always resist efforts of levelers.

Issa: Aha! Now I'm catching on. Though it's true, Basho, that he and I are contemporaries, in temporal terms, that is, but Buson has betrayed his elitism. Haiku as object — hogwash! Each image must reveal what is most human in the heart. I wrote to understand myself, my place in this unsatisfactory world.

Shiki: I'm sitting with my mouth open! Your view of *shasei*, Buson — it seems like a sleepwalker's, who practices without feeling. Where have *you* let your views on aesthetics be known? Truth is, so little was ever known about you . . . you've not shared with the world. Covered your tracks well . . . had quite a job, I'll tell you, trying to trace you.

Buson: What fireworks reticence has kept me from! The world has had all sorts, some who would rather chatter, ruminate or squabble, others who would rather turn their energies to work. You could have found me in my work. I caught a little of another novelty of yours, *rensaku* — sequential composition, as they called it. From what I could gather it led to another serious onslaught of dullness. Was I right in hearing your novices tick off as many as a hundred poems on one subject? Spare us!

Basho: I must say, I agree. In my day, the time of linked verse, the very nature of cooperative quest assured variety, usually giving something of the different sensibilities. Of course the artists were usually gifted, no repetitiveness ever.

Shiki: Linked verse! How disjointed it is to my ear, how lacking . . .

Issa: Wait, let me guess your thought — *makoto*, your "internal reality." Isn't that obvious? Where can you point to a fine poem without it? It was there all the time. Did you think it a discovery?

Shiki: Listen, here's one for the book, an Issa masterpiece:
> One bath
> after another —
> how stupid.

There's profundity for you! Ho, what a choice among internal realities.

Basho: Whoa, my friend. And what of Issa's:
> Where there are humans
> you'll find flies,
> and Buddhas.

To the point, eh?

Issa: I care for some of Shiki's verse, respect his views, whatever he says, but I can't fish among dregs of his infamous excrement spins.

Shiki: A true storm in a *teacup*! Sets your dander up to hear a natural piece on a natural function, eh? I well remember this by *you*:

Raw night air —
horse whinny
steers me to the shithouse.

Buson: Hold it! One can go too far. Some might find such a
subject titillating, but you wouldn't want your art judged by
such cabbage-heads like the Soun lot, forever shouting — and
for what? Indifference to season, abandonment of syllabic con-
straint, their . . .

Shiki: So, was it not great Basho himself who, on occasion,
put his hand to more than seventeen syllables, without
apology? For that, I applaud him. You know his:
　Kareeda ni
　karasu no tomarikeri
　aki no kure
Or as that foreigner out there today might say:
　On the dead limb
　squats a crow —
　autumn night.
Eighteen syllables! Hah! Any complaints? Everyone, as our
good pal taught us, can break fetters.

Basho: On occasion, certainly. But always? Just did a bit of
homework, and came up with facts, Shiki. Out of nine hun-
dred and twenty haiku in one of your collections, one in six
have eighteen or more syllables, and odd as it may seem, when-
ever your tub-thumpers recite them near my stone, I feel they
are among your best. On the other hand, why speak of them
as haiku? I heard someone mention a chat some years ago in
Kyoto between one of Soun's leading poets, the potter Uchi-
jima, and an American from Illinois, wherever that might be,
who had the cockiness to translate all of us into his unimagin-
able tongue. I heard that Uchijima told him why Soun broke
with tradition, that he said precisely, "The old school inhibited
free expression, and they wanted to restore vigor to haiku. It
was in a bad way, little originality, less depth." I'm flabber-

gasted, gentlemen — much of that was attributed to *me*, my name . . .

Buson: And the American's response?

Basho: As I recall, they said he looked extremely puzzled.

Issa: Why could not the potter have been more forthright, spoken of his school's indebtedness, for its most radical program, to Shiki?

Shiki: Out of respect for seniority, no doubt! I approve of his group, we need fresh air.

Basho: Yet there are moderns who haven't strayed that far. They say fiction writers Soseki and Akutagawa . . .

Issa: Soseki's:
    Late cicadas —
    how much longing
    in their song.
A gem!

Shiki: True, you might have come up with that one yourself.
And the so-timely Akutagawa's:
    White chrysanthemums —
    light/dark,
    even their smell.

Buson: Merits its own memorial in this very garden.

Basho: And, Shiki, that devotee of yours, Kyoshi's:
    Insects, village lights,
    longing
    for each other.
How I would love to clasp that poet's hand.

Shiki: And his contemporary, Shuoshi — what spirit!
Kneeling
to a chrysanthemum —
how calm my life.

Issa: Bravo, Shuoshi! A true poet.

Shiki: Another of his might have been inked here, on a day
like this:
Drawing close, I
write in the scent
of chrysanthemums.

Basho: The art will never end! How's this, by Bosha?
Chrysanthemum weather —
shrike
screams from the sky.

Buson: Good poems, all, but in this age exceptions. You can
be rather certain the group scribbling there, practicing *shasei*
no doubt, would be wiser to leave their pages blank. I fear
painting's gone the same way, tradition trampled. Wouldn't be
surprised to see squares, circles, rags, piles of garbage,
splotches of paint without rhyme or reason acclaimed as art
one day. Shiki, your revolution may have set off the beginning
of the end.

Shiki: And that means?

Buson: Surely you must know. The creator will become a dying
breed. Who then will record our joys, our pains?

Issa: How could you not have seen . . .

Shiki: I've always *seen*, always believed in our glorious art.
How can you deny new ages, new talents? Take this poem
by Kasho:

Into the cage of
fireflies, mostly dead,
I send a breath.

Basho, Buson and Issa bow their heads, exclaim in unison:
That strikes a chord!

Shiki: Yes, in spite of all you fear, from time to time art needs
resuscitation, a kick in the pants! Let us drink a final toast to
those yet to come, who will learn something from each one
of us. To haiku!

Sun sets over Hagi-no-Tera as we leave the garden. Trail-
ing my friends, I glance back one last time at the memorial
stones, whisper: To haiku!

MODERN
JAPANESE
HAIKU

SHIKI

(1867–1902)

Such silence:
snow tracing wings
of mandarin ducks.

Midnight sound —
leap up:
a fallen moonflower.

White butterfly
darting among pinks —
whose spirit?

Sudden rain —
rows of horses,
twitching rumps.

Indian summer:
dragonfly shadows seldom
brush the window.

Aged nightingale —
how sweet
the cuckoo's cry.

Autumn come —
cicada husk,
crackling.

Wicker chair
in pinetree's shade,
forsaken.

Evening bell:
persimmons pelt
the temple garden.

           Autumn wind:
           gods, Buddha —
           lies, lies, lies.

Among Saga's
tall weeds,
tombs of fair women.

           Stone
           on summer plain —
           world's seat.

Heath grass —
sandals
still fragrant.

Dew, clinging
to potato field,
the Milky Way.

Summer sky
clear after rain —
ants on parade.

Storm — chestnuts
race along
the bamboo porch.

Imagine —
the monk took off
before the moon shone.

Thing long forgotten —
pot where a flower blooms,
this spring day.

FURA
(1888–1954)

Crow perched
in winter grove —
How far I've come!

HOSHA
(1885–1954)

First thing to catch my ear —
stream
of my native village.

KYOSHI
(1874-1959)

Autumn wind — in my heart,
how many mountains,
how many rivers.

Spring gale —
high on the hill,
I clench my fists.

Millet
of mid-autumn —
my aching back!

How heavy
on my eyes,
the winter sun.

Giant pasania tree,
splitting
autumn's sky.

Lashing wind
parching
the rocks.

Stirring, swaying
in the great sky —
magnolia blossoms.

Insects, village lights,
longing
for each other.

Slighted
by the falcon's eye —
man in the field.

Garden stones,
all day long,
forever.

Beaks of ducks,
dripping
spring mud.

Tossing the may-bug
into the dark —
how deep.

Depth of winter —
every path
twice as long.

> Exiting the Great Gate
> of the harsh Zen temple,
> flower of arrowroot.

Winter trees
lean high
into the heavens.

> Swift boat
> through spring leaves
> tenting the river.

Sick man
squinting through mosquito netting,
into smudge.

Aging —
more haiku,
more turnip broth.

CHIKUREI

(1856–1919)

Indian summer:
twigs of evening sky,
in order.

YAWA

(1895–?)

Flushed faces
of men of Kuzu,
torch-fishing at night.

SOSEKI
(1867–1916)

Late cicadas —
how much longing
in their song.

        Red dragonfly
        seeking company,
        lands on my shoulder.

Winter song —
hatchet felling bamboos
in the mountains.

        Full autumn moon —
        I too am quite well,
        as you see.

Winter blast
drops sun
into the sea.

Echoing
the autumn stream,
a driven stake.

Struck at midday
the wooden fish-shaped gong
spits out mosquitoes.

Which leaves
will be the first to go?
Only the wind knows.

HOSAI

(1885–1926)

Daily, flesh
gets thinner,
bones more thick.

How calming
after rage —
shelling of peas.

Butterfly shadows
all day long,
not a word spoken.

Midnight —
far off
slam of a sliding door.

Loneliness —
my nails grow
longer, longer.

SEIHO
(1899–?)

Nirvana — how dear
through rain
of this troubled world.

HAKUSEN
(20th century)

Night — over
sleeping children,
sound of the waves.

MEISETSU
(1847–1926)

Wind-chime
fresh purchased —
already the town's bell.

        Traveling priest
        vanishing in mist,
        trailed by his bell.

Spring equinox —
beggar, his child
and grandchild.

        From the vast sky,
        pulse
        of starling wings.

All I ask of the world,
a hot water bottle —
I'm cold!

Crossing the bridge —
bright moon
strikes like a gong.

My voice
blown back to me
on autumn wind.

Spring sun,
flies buzzing
around the ink-stone.

Full moon —
barn, stable shadowed
by the plum.

Field tilling
beneath the window —
stones, stones, stones.

Tama river
silvers
the winter moor.

Autumn gale —
tossing sponge cucumber,
shuddering melon.

Spring light
spangling
the peacock.

Splat!
through the sluice-gate,
bellies of frogs.

SUIHA
(1872–1946)

Steady
autumn wind,
mosquito swatter.

Postman — how high
will he climb into
snow-drifts of mountains?

Under pine-cones
ripples
of summer rain.

Violets —
rays of sunlight,
reclaimed.

DAKOTSU
(1885–1962)

Death at last —
little by little
fading of medicine odors.

                              Into the nostrils
                              of the corpse,
                              autumn wind.

The iron wind-chime
rings
autumn in.

                              Mountain
                              shadowing mountain,
                              dew on a Taro leaf.

SEISENSUI
(1884–?)

My truths:
Buddha, green
ears of barley.

> Butterfly kidnapped
> from butterfly —
> all's a-flutter.

Evening grave —
footprint
on trodden earth.

> Full moon
> come to
> its glorious end.

Winter evening —
shadow and I,
writing about me.

Snow falling
in and out
the water.

In mountain sky
a line of smoke —
someone lives up there.

SANTOKA

(1882–1940)

Song of the river
leads me
to my village.

To the end of time,
journeying,
cutting toe-nails.

Laying down chopsticks —
enough.
I'm grateful.

Dragonfly
perched on my shoulder,
out for a stroll.

Tramping farther,
farther —
one green hill after another.

SHIKUNRO

(20th century)

Beggar passes —
shadow to sunlight,
sunlight to shadow.

GOMEI

(20th century)

July — already
autumn wind
is in the rain.

SEISI
(1869–1937)

The beggar
whisks the butterfly
before him.

Frozen together
in one dream —
sea-slugs.

Autumn wind —
fishes stock-still
in the deep.

Even housebound
the winter fly
follows the sun.

NISSHO

(20th century)

Sweet-meat seller
leaves the town,
sky filling his breast.

TOYOJO
(1878–?)

Brow to cliff,
he drinks
clear water.

KOYO
(1867–1903)

Any chance it's in Chuang Tzu,
this green bird's
floating nest?

                    Sudden shower
                    on my face — nine gallons
                    of lust rinsed off.

FUSEI
(1885-?)

Looking back —
evening cherry blossoms
farther, farther.

Through petals
on the pond,
eye of the frog.

Cat dozing on the stove —
is there one thing
he doesn't know?

HOSHA

(20th century)

Pitched into
autumn sunlight,
rocks of Kiso Valley.

KAFUGEN
(20th century)

Striking the sick man
off to find help,
thin shadows of trees.

HEKIGODO
(1873–1937)

Oranges
dyeing the wall,
painting the slope.

Winter storm —
at the stone wall
a drift of ducks.

All that God offers —
this path across
the parched moor.

Late spring rain —
again I must become
just me.

SUJU
(1893–?)

Ladybird takes off,
wings
parting her in two.

                    Water birds,
                    busy drawing lines
                    between themselves.

Even at night
leaves cascade
to the walk.

CHOHA
(20th century)

In the haze —
the vesper's bell,
scent of the hedge.

ICHIO
(20th century)

Wind reeling by —
how bright,
how clear.

KUSATAO
(1901–?)

Town sky —
one new thing,
the swallows.

Suddenly
remembering her,
his feet crushed gravel.

With autumn
both grown old,
my friend, the door-plate.

Autumn sun —
dead friend's hand
warm on my shoulder.

With spring leaves,
my child's
new teeth.

Glimmering across
the railroad tracks,
white socks.

Horse, carting
winter sunlight
on his back.

HOSAKU
(1906-1936)

Out at sea,
lungs ride
cold blue.

                    Noonday sun —
                    how lonely,
                    my shadow.

FUKIO
(1903–1930)

Mid-winter — crow
drops down
on its own shadow.

TAKEO
(1908–?)

Waterfall dried up,
moonlight
drenches the rocks.

                            Sunrise at sea —
                            cock cries,
                            breath pluming.

Sick of earth,
lark rises, singing,
from the heart.

                            Low spring tide —
                            every thing
                            grained with sand.

Talking stops —
white petals
falling in my heart.

KYOHO
(20th century)

Mackerel sky—
reminding me
of long ago.

HAKUU
(1911–1936)

Cricket chirp —
now
my life is clear.

SHUOSHI

(1892–?)

Meadow woodpecker,
quickening
the fall of leaves.

                    Wild roses drenched
                    in morning rain,
                    as in a casting net.

Kneeling
to a chrysanthemum —
how calm my life.

                    Drawing close, I
                    write in the scent
                    of chrysanthemums.

SHIHAKU
(20th century)

Again, blood from
my lungs — how clear
my loved ones' faces.

GENZABURO

(20th century)

Children somersaulting
into winter sky—
no bribe from anyone.

HAKYO
(1913-1969)

Fallen leaves —
white hands of invalids
round the bonfire.

           Spring hurricane —
           yet the ghost
           ventures out.

Crane carries
my passion
into the autumn night.

           Left by
           the firefly,
           grass bends low.

SHOKEISHI

(20th century)

Mountain mist
tints the whirlpool
of the dam.

BOSHA
(1900–1941)

Rain stopped,
whirligig once more
rainbowed with light.

> New grass —
> gently, gently
> I tread on clouds.

Horse —
up to its ears
in radishes.

> Herb gatherer —
> baby on her back
> becomes a stone.

Autumn morn —
dew on the Taro leaf
fades in air.

Chrysanthemum weather —
shrike
screams from the sky.

Midwinter horsetail —
yum!
I am Saint Epicurus.

A fit of coughing
spoils
the song of pines.

Leaving me,
my cough tears
through the woods.

From the heavens,
silently snowing,
shrill of the kite.

SHINKICHI
(1901–1987)

My hair's falling fast —
this afternoon
I'm off to Asia Minor.

> Of all things living
> I'd be a sweet potato,
> fresh dug up.

I'm cheerful, whatever happens,
a puff in sky —
what splendor exists, I'm there.

> Just say, "He's out"—
> back in
> five billion years!

HAKUCHIN

(20th century)

Dozing in the boat
under the river of heaven,
miles from home.

SEKITO

(20th century)

Autumn storm —
faces drawing close
in candle-light.

SOJO
(1901-1956)

Nightwatchman
strikes the hour,
cracking the moon.

        Fever gone,
        the void
        a sickly yellow.

Seeds spread
on my palm,
quaking with life.

        Flame passing
        from stick to stick —
        such quiet.

My wife — blurred
in my right eye,
clear in my left.

TAIZO
(20th century)

Cloudy noon —
the garden peony,
how deeply white.

KEION
(1877–1927)

Cherry blossoms,
against
a drape of cloud.

Man strolls
unheedingly
through cries of insects.

SEKITEI

(1886-1951)

In two corners
of my temple garden
insects carry on.

Imagining sleet
pelting
on my corpse.

SHACHIKU
(1872–1913)

Winter blast —
crow droppings
white on stones.

IPPEKIRO
(1887–1946)

Looking up —
how still
the tree I cut.

> Green barley —
> come dawn,
> what scurrying.

In the stable,
meek, quiet, the horse
that killed the farmer.

AKUTAGAWA
(1892–1927)

Frog, so green —
are you
fresh painted?

                        Winter wind —
                        sardine's still
                        ocean-colored.

White chrysanthemums —
light/dark,
even their smell.

YOFU
(20th century)

Night cherry blossoms
tinted
by the bonfire.

KASHO
(20th century)

I live with Buddha,
but when cold
I long for mortals.

Into the cage of
fireflies, mostly dead,
I send a breath.

SEISU
(1892–?)

Wild boar
hooked up there,
heavy with snow.

HAJIME
(20th century)

Bird song —
a thin dust
on the piano.

FUJIO

(20th century)

How gracefully
cows trample
fields of violets.

UTSUJI
(1881–1920)

Socks drying
in frosty sun —
brrr!

Evening thought,
burning rubbish,
ear cocked for the nightingale.

SEISHI
(1901–?)

Faster, faster —
whorled shell
of the snail.

Moonlight —
frozen
in mid-air.

Here at the crossroads,
everywhere,
same autumn dusk.

Cricket —
with every chirp
the house grows older.

Dead thrush,
leaving me
to spread its wings.

Smelting furnace,
under the green
mountain of July.

With every cry
of the shrike,
I know I am.

Praying mantis
straddling a wasp —
how crisp each bite.

In this wasted field
here in my palm —
sunset.

Dangling in
summer river,
a red iron chain.

Deepening my grief,
snap
of a branch.

Dewy night,
blazing stars —
I'll live forever.

Where has it flown,
snowcap
of Mount Ibuki?

Keeping snow at bay —
fence
of the Zen Hall.

I stopped —
the stream
flowed off alone.

Long have I
used it, body
damp with dew.

As long as I stand
on the cliff edge,
crabs stay put.

TATSUKO
(20th century)

Winter light
touches the Great Buddha,
then the hills.

ARO
(1879–1951)

Reaching for the heart
of spring —
wind from tree to tree.

Winter fly —
clinging to grass,
withering together.

SHIZUNOJO

(20th century)

Cold night — before
the mirror
in the stillness of her skirt.

ICHIRINSO
(20th century)

A bit of sun —
world's full
of drying socks.

SANKI
(1900–1962)

Great drought —
first a brown cow,
then its moo.

Come May, more and more
the dog
smells like dog.

SEISETSU
(1871–1917)

Sea-slug, what kind
of Buddha
will you be?

MOKKOKU
(1889–?)

Through
the scoop-net,
moon-drops.

                         From the branch
                         petals drifting
                         by the moon.

RINKA

(1904–?)

Butterflies gone,
how sharply blue
the sky.

Anniversary
of my father's death —
snow shrouds the charcoal.

KIJO
(1865-1938)

Rice-field path —
tempting cat's claws,
the swallows.

Tillers of earth
living, dying,
dying, living.

Dying grasshopper,
grasping
a clod of earth.

Winter brook —
flowering on a pebble,
a sprig of water.

Spring rain —
could it be
the ghost of stones.

SHUSON
(1905–?)

Over the mantis
I cup my hand —
a mantis.

Trees lost in haze —
a glint far off
becomes a heron.

KAKIO
(1902–1962)

Coughing into
leafless trees —
the sky coughs back.

                           Dried reeds —
                           I cart them home,
                           in my eyes.

TOTA
(20th century)

After hateful words,
I roar off
like a motorcycle.

Feels at home
here in the slums,
the butterfly.

Red smoke lifts
from the steel mill —
a tired arm.